# THE STREET NAMES OF HAWORTH

# Street Names
## *of*
# Haworth

by
Jennie
Crawford

Wharncliffe Publishing

*In memory of my father*

First Published in 1998 by
**Wharncliffe Publishing**
**an imprint of**
**Pen and Sword Books Limited,**
**47 Church Street, Barnsley,**
**South Yorkshire S70 2AS**

Copyright © Wharncliffe Publishing, 1998

*For up-to-date information on other titles produced under the
Wharncliffe imprint, please telephone or write to:*

**Wharncliffe Publishing**
**FREEPOST**
**47 Church Street**
**Barnsley**
**South Yorkshire S70 2BR**
**Telephone (24 hours): 01226 - 734555**

## ISBN: 1-871647-47-9

A CIP catalogue record of this book is available from the
British Library

Printed in Great Britain by
Redwood Books, Trowbridge, Wiltshire

# CONTENTS

*Looking down Main Street, Haworth.*

# Introduction

**D**o you live on a road, terrace, lane, way or street? Or perhaps your street may be an avenue, close, gardens or mews?

Have you ever stopped to wonder about the special meaning of your street's name? You may be surprised at the history which is revealed: the name may conjure up pictures from a distant past, or provide clues to a different life long ago, when people were closer to the land and the land's features were most important to a largely rural community. Some names often found in the Haworth area are 'Royd' (meaning cleared woodland), 'Birks' (meaning birch trees) and 'Ebor' (which refers to the wild boar found hereabouts in times past). Other names refer to events like battles of the Crimean War, and to Queen Victoria and her family.

The history of British roads goes back to the Bronze and Iron Ages, when tracks became formed to link settlements. Britain was a wild and inhospitable country of thick forests, swampy ground

*Roads of the Haworth area in 1771, from Thomas Jefferys' Survey of the County of York.*

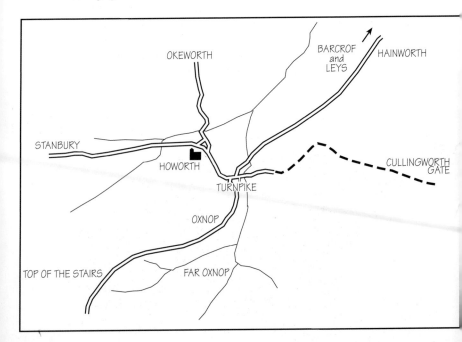

and rough terrain. Tribes wandered the country looking for a place to settle: the tracks were used by invaders, travellers and traders. The long distance tracks linked settlements, often keeping to the high ground. After the Roman conquest, many of the tracks were improved, and new roads built which were paved, ditched and cambered. The names of the Roman roads are Saxon in origin - the word 'street' refers to a paved road, whereas a 'way' was any route which had evolved - usually a wide, grassy track.

Evidence may be seen of the different types of route which developed all over the country according to need: pack horse routes, smugglers ways, green ways and burial ways. Many of them started as simple farm tracks linking villages and churches with outlying farms and hamlets. The Turnpike Trusts, like Haworth's Blue Bell Trust and the Lees and Hebden Bridge Trust were surfaced toll roads set up to carry materials like raw cotton from Manchester, spun yarn to Lancashire, coal, coaches and post services.

Before the industrial revolution, most street names evolved from descriptions of the locality, and these are often linked to local field names. Lord Lane, Sike Lane and Stubbing Lane refer in turn to the Lord's ownership, a watercourse and a clearing. Gate is a Danish word meaning 'street' (as in Cook Gate - where cooked food might be sold).

After the industrial revolution, with the huge expansion in industry and urban housing, streets were named purposefully, and there was an Act of Parliament to enforce this. Names celebrated landowners, explorers and new locations to be proud of (Fairfax Street, Nares Street, Station Road and Drill Street).

Later in the nineteenth century, many streets were also named after Queen Victoria and royalty (Victoria Road, Prince Street, Regent Street), names of famous battles (Alma Street) and patriotic figures (Nelson Street, Stanley Street). Other topics were local flora and fauna, and Christian names which often related to a landowner or builder's family.

In the twentieth century, it became popular to use words like Avenue, Drive, View, Crescent, Grove, Mews and Way, and new developments were likely to bear the names of trees, rivers, flowers and other country connections thought to bestow an air of gentility and rural calm (as in Laburnum Grove).

A new and encouraging trend, seen recently in Oxenhope, is for builders to request research into an area to find out what local names are important and could be used, before naming a new road.

To delve into the fascinating subject of street names and their meanings is to raise more questions than can be answered in a brief overview. This book is not meant as a final text - not all names are included - but I hope to raise the reader's interest and encourage further investigation. Many names are open to interpretation, and the author has tried to suggest meanings which might be logical and useful as a starting point for further research. Any comments on the text would be very much welcomed, and hopefully incorporated into later editions.

The derivation of names, where appropriate, has been taken from A.E. Smith's book *Place names of the West Riding. English Place-Name Society, 1961.*

*Old route to Hebden Bridge via Top of Stairs.*

# Haworth in the Past

Looking around Haworth today, the grey stone village on its steep hillside is crowded with visitors from all over the world, the main centres of interest being the Parsonage and the cobbled main street. Many tourists will not seek to explore further than the Brontë connection. However, for anyone who cares to look beyond, clues to a more distant past may be followed, and it is not hard to imagine the humble beginnings of the early hill village and the harsh climate in which it developed. Haworth's name most probably means 'the hedged (or high) farmstead', coming from Old English words for a farm as a 'hedged enclosure', which would be perched on the slope of this windy and exposed hillside.

*Main Street, Haworth circa 1905.*

*View of Haworth from the Brow.*

The original farm clung to the hill in bleak and barren surroundings: there may be a Saxon site where Changegate is today, although Haworth is not mentioned in the Domesday Survey. The hill village developed slowly. Isolated amongst the moors, it was only reached with difficulty by hardy pack horses whose owners had often driven them against the elements to cross the Pennines, or negotiated the tough 'Stairs' route from the Manchester direction. The tracks wound out of the village across the bleak and beautiful moors to Lancashire, to Hebden Bridge, to Bradford and to the nearest civilisation downstream - Keighley, six miles distant.

**Early street layout**

The 1852 Ordnance Survey map shows clearly the layout of the main streets. The oldest lanes, which also appear in outline on the 1771 Jefferys map (except the Hebden Bridge Trust), were Mytholme Lane, Lord Lane (via Cook Gate), Sike Lane (now Belle Isle Road and Mill Hey), the Blue Bell Trust (West Lane) which led to Lancashire, Stubbing Lane and the Lees and Hebden Bridge Trust 1814. Many local names on this map still remain today: five worsted mills bearing watery or rural names; Springhead, Bridge House, Mytholme ('where streams join'), Hollins ('holly') and Ebor ('boar'). Other colourful local names, like Brandy Row, have disappeared.

As original settlements were often on hilltops, so Haworth houses cluster around the church, with smaller communities in family or farm groups (the word 'fold' often denotes an old farmstead). As the industrial eighteenth century progressed, houses were built alongside main roads. This can be seen in the long, steep main street where cottages were built down each side (where possible) to link with cottage communities and mills in the valley.

Haworth was growing in importance as a centre in the area for worsted spinning and weaving, and therefore reliable communications became increasingly necessary during the eighteenth and nineteenth centuries, leading to an improved road system and the building of the railway in 1857. However, the main street remained very much as it appears today - the stone setts laid on edge down its length and around the church, were vital to stop horses with carts from slipping on the dangerous gradient.

## Disasters and the Township Folk

Haworth inhabitants had to endure far more than isolation and harsh winters. Difficulties of access to the village were made far worse by the vagaries of climate. By the seventeenth century, the parish records were relating a tale of bleak hardship, disaster and tragedy for the villagers. On 17th July, 1646, there was 'a great tempest, with thunder and lightnings, such as few have ever seen'. In 1649, a great fall of snow lasted until the last week of winter, and on February 25th 1649, two illusory suns appeared on either side of the sun. The drought year 1652 culminated in 'a storm of wind and hail, some shaped like spur rowels' – this was thought to be the effect of the conjunction of Saturn and Mars in Leo. Another long drought in 1681 set fire to the moors.

Nearly a century later, the village folk were still being traumatised by cataclysmic events: a powerful earthquake in 1757 and a putrid fever which killed many during 1763, as they struggled to make a living in the bleak and barren country.

## The coming of the Bronte family

In 1820 the Reverend Brontë brought the trap containing his wife and six children, (with all their furniture on two flat carts, according to an eyewitness), over the 8 miles of rough lanes from Thornton. It is thought they travelled over the hilly route via Oxenhope to climb the steep main street up to the Parsonage. Haworth had 4,668 inhabitants in 1821, many of whom were employed in the mills. The novelist Mrs Gaskell, describes how the village was built with no regard to sanitation: 'The great old churchyard lies above the houses, and it is terrible to think how the very water-springs of the pumps below must be poisoned'.

We receive a melancholy picture from the Brontës of the winter of 1833/4 being particularly wet and dreary, with an unusual number of deaths in the village - funeral bells tolling, the chipping of the masons cutting gravestones in a nearby shed. There were several inns, however, to provide relief for some inhabitants!

In 1848 there was an influenza epidemic: Branwell Bronte died, and the next year, his sister Anne.

The Babbage Report of 1850 painted a horrifying picture of the state of sanitation in the village, with streets being used as drains, and water unfit to drink, and this was a signal for the beginning of general improvements in public health which continued into the twentieth century.

*Church Street (formerly Parsonage Lane)*

# *Turnpikes and Nuisances*

The Turnpike Trusts were set up to try and improve road communications between the expanding industrial towns. The dreadful state of the roads, which were often only passable by pack animals, made it impossible to operate an effective transport system for goods and raw materials.

There were particular problems in the Bradford and Pennine districts, due to the steep hills and unpredictable weather. Landowners along the routes formed the membership of the Trusts and toll keepers collected the revenue, usually calculated on the number of animals pulling a vehicle and taking into account such details as width of wheel rim and number of milestones in a section. However, collecting the revenue was extremely difficult, as people tried to find different routes to avoid paying and would often refuse to pay. A toll gate was erected on West Lane in 1759, but had moved by 1763 to Main Street, opposite the Black Bull, in an attempt to stop avoidance. By 1800, however, it had returned to West Lane.

There was also a Toll Gate House and toll bars at the bottom of Main Street, blocking off what are now Sun Street and Bridgehouse Lane. Other Toll Houses were at Mytholmes Lane and Haworth Brow.

The Turnpike Act for the road through Haworth from Colne

## ROAD IMPROVEMENTS IN THE HAWORTH AREA BY 1815

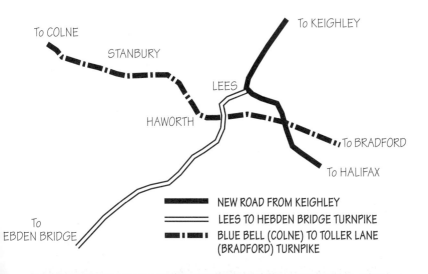

To COLNE

STANBURY

To KEIGHLEY

LEES

HAWORTH

To BRADFORD

To HALIFAX

To
EBDEN BRIDGE

▬▬▬ NEW ROAD FROM KEIGHLEY
═══ LEES TO HEBDEN BRIDGE TURNPIKE
▬ ▪ ▬ ▪ ▬ BLUE BELL (COLNE) TO TOLLER LANE (BRADFORD) TURNPIKE

*Old turnpike road over the Pennines to Lancashire.*

to Bradford was passed in 1755. This is likely to have been an original pack route over the Pennines from medieval times. It was called the Blue Bell, Haworth and Toller Lane Road, Blue Bell being the starting point on the edge of Colne. This was a wild and treacherous road, liable to be blocked with snow, and climbing to the Herders' Inn, at 1,127 ft with an arduous trek over the high moors and a series of twists and steep dives before the climb to Haworth.

The Act for the Lees to Hebden Bridge Road was passed in 1814. The original pack route to Hebden Bridge ran from Lees to Bridge House, up the steep hill to Hall Green and along Stubbing Lane to Old Oxenhope and Leeshaw. The rough road can be seen clearly, climbing steeply up the hill side to cross the moor, before descending to join the present road near Pecket Well. This is a delightful walking route today.

*Site of the Toll House at the junction of Main Street, Sun Street and Bridgehouse Lane, with the Old Hall middle left.*

*Bottom of Main Street, from the site of the Toll House.*

There were complaints about the narrowness of the Bridgehouse bridge in 1767, and in the same year, Sladen bridge was rebuilt and the road widened. With the improvements in the roads, came more traffic, and even more need for continuous improvement.

In 1815, there was a daily service coach which ran direct from Manchester to Keighley via Rochdale, Todmorden and Hebden Bridge, taking five hours. The new coach was the 'Enterprise' as advertised by the *Leeds Mercury* on 28th October of that year.

## NUISANCES

### Complaints about the 'bad state of the roads' and other 'nuisances'

By the 1870s, efforts were being made to keep the Haworth roads in a state of repair. At the extraordinary monthly meeting of the Haworth Local Board of Health on 6 June, 1871, it was resolved 'that the new road from Lees Syke to Brow Bar be repaired ...having recommended that the Surveyors post bills inviting tenders for getting, leading and breaking stones required for repairing roads... and that 100 yards in length of new setting be done in the Main Street'.

However, improvements were not happening fast enough, as

15

seen in the minutes of the Haworth Local Board. On 1st August, 1871, the Clerk read out a letter from the Crabtree Brothers of Oxenhope, wishing to call the Surveyor's attention to the bad state of the road from Lees Syke to Hauckliff, 'as it is in a most dangerous state for travelling at present, and if you do not attend to it at once we shall be obliged to summon you without further notice'.

Barely a month passed before there was another complaint, this time from Mr William Ferrand of St. Ives, Bingley. Apparently, some workmen had been relaying the surface and had carelessly left the road in such a state that '...I broke my carriage in passing over it...I have been obliged to send it to the coachmakers, and when it is repaired I shall ... require payment by the Haworth Local Board'.

These weighty matters had all to be dealt with by the Board, along with reports from the Nuisance Inspector regarding 'very bad smells' and 'nuisances', including a certain James Smith of Main Street, who persisted in keeping poultry in his house. It had, however, been resolved in May 1871 that the streets be swept once a week 'and the refuse be removed the same day and deposited in such a place that it shall not cause a nuisance'.

A further contentious issue was that the Toll was still in operation. The Clerk to the Oxenhope District Local Board discovered from the *Leeds Mercury* that the Toll on the Lees and Hebden Bridge Turnpike Road was to be continued, and wrote a furious letter to the Board about this 'obnoxious impost', being strongly convinced that 'this is unneccessary, and that steps should be taken at least for an investigation into the pecuniary affairs of the said Trust'. The Haworth Board Clerk merely replied that nothing could be done until the Trust had expired.

# *Local Names in Brontë Times*

These are names of streets, crofts, inns, houses and fields from the Haworth Rate Books from 1833 - 1848. The Reverend Patrick Brontë is listed as incumbent at the Parsonage. Many of the names listed appear later in street names. From the Tithe Award (1852), we can see the name of Patrick Brontë, A.B., and also Arthur B. Nicholls, Curate, resident in the Sexton's House, together with John Brown, stone cutter. Haworth residents at this time pursued occupations such as handloom weaver, woolcomber, farmer, wool carder, stone mason, power loom weaver, 'parish relief', master carpenter, clog maker, tea dealer and stationer, Chelsea Pensioner, cartwright, barber and a variety of others.

*Church Street (formerly Parsonage Lane).*

## Local Names

| | | |
|---|---|---|
| Gauger Croft | Parsonage Croft | Copy |
| Lion Inn | Stubbing (Lane) | Newsholmes Mill |
| Cook Gate | Townend | Ginnel |
| Mill Hey | Fold | Belle Isle |
| Hall | Woodlands | King's Arms |
| Sun House | Chapel House | Valenciennes (houses) |
| Haworth Brow | Heys | Ebor |
| Mill Bridge | Mill Hill | Moor End |
| Hawkcliffe | Bridge House | Folly |
| Bunker's Hill | Ducking Stool | Dyke |
| Sowdens | Balcony | Parsonage Lane |
| Howdens | Hob Nook | Sun |
| Town Field | Mytholmes | Pennistone |
| West Lane | Old Field Gate | Rough Nook |
| Hollings | Top of the Hill | Dallow Moor |
| Intake | Springs | Lower Laith |
| Mat Coat | Henfield Side | New Mill |
| Spout Stones | Lord Wood | New Road Side (1845/1848) |
| Bank | Greenfield House | |

The streets which appear in the Tithe Award of 1852 are Church Street, West Lane, Fold, Ginnel, Well Lane, Well Street, Townend, Back Lane, Mytholmes Lane, the Hebden Road (Turnpike Road) and other unnamed 'public roads'.

It is interesting to speculate on the local families and traders who might have been known by the Brontë family, like John Brown, stonecutter, (with premises on each side of the National School on Parsonage Lane), Thomas Parker, grocer and mason and William Hartley, iron monger, neighbours next but one to the church gates. Robert Lambert, druggist, lived in the shop which turns at an angle, opposite the church gates. A butcher's shop occupied by William Garnett stood at the junction of Changegate (Ginnel) and West Lane, where the Tourist Information Centre is now located. Further down Main Street were the shoe maker, draper, clock maker, carpenter, wine and spirit merchant and several more grocers and butchers. Ann Sugden, school mistress, lived in Gauger's Croft, and the house of Edward South Hall, surgeon, was a little way along West Lane, just past the Fold.

# Nineteenth Century Expansion

The nineteenth century was a time of great industrial change. The boom in industry brought families from the land to work in the textile mills and new houses were needed to accommodate them.

In the early part of the century, the rate of change in new streets and buildings appears fairly slow. Haworth Rate Books from 1833 - 1838 record names of fields, crofts, buildings and their owners. Some streets are named, for example Ginnel, Mill Hey, Gauger Croft (1833), Mill Hill, Bunker's Hill (1838), Stubbing Lane, Bunker's Hill, West Lane (1842) and New Road Side (1845).

*View of Hall Green streets of textile workers' houses from Haworth Brow.*

The Census Returns from 1841 to 1891 provide a fascinating record of Haworth inhabitants, their families and occupations. Names of streets were gradually included as these developed, particularly as the township expanded in the latter half of the nineteenth century. It is particularly interesting to see the huge increase in the number of streets which occurred between 1871 and 1891.

### The 1841 Census

The 1841 Census return shows a picture of what Haworth's street plan would have been like generally from early times, with the layout changing gradually over the years as farms and folds developed to accommodate families of workers, and houses were built along the main thoroughfares for traders and handloom weavers. Along with farms, groups of cottages and important houses, such as the

*Streets of textile workers' houses in Haworth Brow.*

Parsonage, the following lanes and thoroughfares are listed:

| | |
|---|---|
| Upper Mill Hill | Parsonage Lane |
| Mill Hey | West Lane |
| Lower Mill Hill | Back Lane |
| Bunkers Hill | Well Lane |
| Stubbing Lane | Ginnel |

Gauger's Croft (Although not strictly a lane, this area is included as it covers a warren of houses and warehouses later named as streets)

## The 1851 Census

Several names are listed for the first time, these being as follows:

| | |
|---|---|
| Haworth Brow | Main Street |
| Back of Main Street | Church Street |
| Roper Square (in Gauger's Croft) | Newall Hill |
| Principal Street (part of Main Street) | Butt Lane Top |
| Brigg Lane (Main Street from the Fleece Inn downwards) | |

## The 1861 and 1871 Census returns.

In the 1861 census, only two new street names are listed, these being New Road Side and Parson Lane (Previously Parsonage Lane). Church Street, Ebor Lane Top and Mytholmes Lane were new names in 1871 (although the name of Mytholmes was not new), together with Albert Terrace. The people living on the new Albert Terrace were the Soothill, Smith, Mitchell and Townsend families, and their occupations were cabinet maker, outdoor labourer, machine woolcomber and wool sorter.

## The 1881 Census

In 1881, the picture is changing dramatically, as new roads were being built at Haworth Brow, to cope with the industrial expansion and need for workers' housing. Many new houses have been built along New Road Side. Back Lane has changed its name to North Street and Changegate has replaced Ginnel.

The new and re-named roads listed on the 1881 census are as follows:

| | |
|---|---|
| Clarendon Road | Lord Street |
| Duke Street | Clarance Street |
| Victoria Road | Grosvenor Street |
| Aire Street | Ivy Bank Lane |

Ouse Street                                               Kirkgate
Low Street (the lower part of Main Street) Cripple Lane (off Main Street)
North Street                                             Changegate(Low Changegate)
Cook Gate Lane                                       Ashmount Place


**The 1891 Census**
By the 1891 census, whole blocks of streets had been built at
Haworth Brow. Although some of the streets have now
disappeared, it is interesting to see on the census where small
groups of streets have related names. We can see flocks of birds,
groups of trees and plants, family names, rivers and royalty.

The following streets at Haworth Brow are named for the first
time on the census return:

| | | | |
|---|---|---|---|
| Lark Street | Hebden Road | Prince Street | John Street |
| Jay Street | Apsley Street | Park Street | Lot Street |
| Rook Street | Dean Street | Bright Street | Emily Street |
| Dove Street | Carlton Street | Oak Street | Jane Street |
| Wren Street | Cliffe Street | River Street | Ann Street |
| Brow Road | Fife Street | May Street | Thomas Street |
| Station Road | | | |

Continuing this theme on the Haworth side of Bridgehouse Beck,
but also noting that many of the 'streets' named were already in
existence as groups of cottages, the new street names on the 1891
census are as follows:

| | | | |
|---|---|---|---|
| Fig Street | Belle Isle Rd. | Queen Street | Minnie Street |
| Lindon Street | Prospect St. | Earl Street | Back Minnie St. |
| Pine Street | Hall Street | Clarendon St. | Shirley Street |
| Fir Street | Sun Street | King Street | Hird Street |
| Fern Street | Moon Street | Bank Street | Gibb Street |
| Ivy Street | Croft Street | Top Street | Acton Street |
| Roper Street | Little Street | Mount Street | Back Street |
| Cork Street | Nth. View Ter. | Star Street | Hollings Hill |

Lodge Street (previously Newall Hill)

## Acre Lane

An acre was taken as the area a yoke of oxen could plough in a day. The original meaning was unenclosed land, later changing to tilled or enclosed land. Acre Lane is said to be very close to the first croft which worked all the land around Haworth from early times, and borders the Acre field (Ref. 561, 1852 Tithe Award).

## Aire Street

Two river-named streets lie close to River Street, on the banks of Bridgehouse Beck. The name 'Aire' has watery derivations, although there is much discussion over the precise meaning. It may be a British word which translates as 'strong river', or the Old British and Irish words for 'water', or the Old English 'river, stream', or the Old English 'an island, land partly surrounded by water', or Old Norse for 'sandbank'. Similar Latin and French words for 'water' complete the choice.

See Appendix, for some other Haworth streets with a river theme, e.g. Lune Street and Ouse Street.

## Albion Street

Albion was said to be the ancient native name for the island of Britain. The word has been translated as meaning 'the white land', a reference to the white cliffs of Dover. The patriotic Victorians held the figure of Albion as a symbol of the spirit of

*Main Street Haworth, c.1893*

the age, thus continuing the theme of exploration and discovery in this group of Lees street names.

See also other Lees streets on the theme of exploration and empire: Cecil Street, Douglas Street, Gordon Street, Nares Street, Nile Street, Stanley Street.

## Alice Street
Princess Alice (b. 1843), was one of Queen Victoria's nine children, and later became Grand Duchess of Hesse.

## Alma Street
The Battle of the Alma (September, 1854) was one of the great battles of the Crimean War (1854 - 1856). The Alma Heights had to be captured from the Russians, as they barred the way to Sebastopol. About 2,000 British troops were killed out of a force of 27,000 British, 30,000 French and 7,000 Turks. The war in the Crimea brought back popular support for the monarchy, as Queen Victoria took an active interest. She was seen to support Florence Nightingale's work, visiting injured soldiers and instituting the Victoria Cross for gallantry in action.

## Ann Street
There are several female Christian names amongst the Haworth streets: others are May Street, Minnie Street, Shirley Street and Ruth Street. This 'Ann' may refer to the famous sister, Anne Brontë (1820-1849), or, stretching the imagination, even to the great Lady Anne Clifford, Countess of Dorset, Pembroke and

*Ann Street.*

Montgomery, who was born at Skipton Castle, and lived at the time of the Civil War. Streets were also often named after the builder or landowner's family perhaps his wife, daughter or son. James Bottomley of Greenfield (previously of Prince Street), was given permission for 5 houses and a shop on Ann and Carlton Streets in 1895, and for 6 houses on Ann Street in 1902.

See Appendix for other streets relating to female Christian names.

### Apsley Street

The name Apsley means 'apple trees in a clearing'. The street dates from 1890.

### Arctic Street

Anyone who has observed Arctic Street in a snowstorm would agree that it is appropriately named. However, Arctic exploration was in the news in the latter half of the nineteenth century, and there are connections with two neighbouring Lees streets, Nelson Street and Nares Street. An early expedition of Lord Nelson's was to the Arctic, while in 1875-76 Sir George Strong Nares captained an expedition to the Arctic in the vessels 'Alert' and 'Discovery'.

See also: Nares Street, Nelson Street.

*Arctic Street.*

## Ash Street

A number of streets in the locality are named after trees native to the north of England. The beautiful native mountain ash, with its red berries in season, is a common sight growing wild in this area, due to its liking for hilly land with well drained soil. The name comes from an Old Norse word.

See Appendix for some other Haworth streets named after trees, e.g. Fir Street, Lime Street, Oak Street and Pine Street.

## Ashfield Terrace

The word 'field' originally meant a broad clearing free of trees, (in this case ash trees). It gradually evolved into today's understanding as an enclosed piece of land.

## Baden Street

Robert, 1st Lord Baden-Powell, led the defence of Mafeking, which he held for 215 days (1899-1900), and became a national hero. He was founder of the Boy Scout movement in 1908.

Messrs Bottomley and Sunderland were granted permission to build 16 houses on Baden Street in 1899.

## Barcroft

The Bercroft family were Haworth landowners, heirs of John de Haworth. Godfrey de Haworth, Roger de Manyngham and Alicia de Bercroft owned four oxgangs of land in Haworth, according to 'Kirkby's Inquest' (1296). This is the first recorded mention of the name Haworth, which does not appear in the Domesday survey. The name Bercroft means 'barley enclosure'.

## Belle Isle Road

Belle Isle appears as a field name (Ref. 556, 1852 Tithe Awards), and the present road is built across the field from Bridgehouse Lane. In 1838, Belle Isle field, together with Corn Mill, were owned by the executors of Richard Emmott Esq., and tenanted by Robert Murgatroyd. The Emmott family were still owners in 1852. Belle Isle Road led across the Mill Bridge to Mill Hey, before the railway and Station Road were built.

The name probably originates from the Strait of Belle Isle, which connects the Gulf of St. Lawrence in Canada with the Atlantic, and refers to the victorious British and American campaign which ended in the capture of Quebec from the French

*Belle Isle Road.*

by James Wolfe in 1759.

It is interesting that the British also occupied the French island of Belle-Ile-en Mer, off the south west coast of Brittany, from 1761 to 1763.

### Branwell Drive

The Branwell name is famous for its Brontë family connections. Maria Branwell of Penzance married the Reverend Patrick Brontë in 1812. Patrick Branwell, their only son, was born in Thornton in 1817. After Maria died in 1821, her elder sister Elizabeth Branwell came from Cornwall to look after the children. Although she had doted on Patrick Branwell as a child, and helped to pay for his art education, Miss Branwell left him out of her will because of his reckless spending and dissolute habits. He died in 1848, aged 30 years.

See Appendix for some other streets with 'Brontë' interest e.g. Brontë Street, Emily Street and Heath-Cliff.

### Bridgehouse Lane

Bridgehouse is first documented in 1596 (Court Rolls of the Manor of Haworth), and again in 1656 as Brigghouse, when the Parish Records note that the bridge was repaired with new timber and stone heads, after a continually wet summer the previous year. Bridgehouse Lane formed part of the Blue Bell Trust (Bradford to Colne) turnpike road. Bridgehouse Mill was

28

established around 1788, and carried out cotton spinning, worsted spinning and combing.

**Bright Street**
John Bright (1811-1889) was a nineteenth century reformer and Liberal statesman, MP at various times for Durham, Manchester and Birmingham. He founded the Anti-Corn Law League with Richard Cobden. They were both publicly against the war in the Crimea - but this was not a popular view and mobs burnt effigies of the two in the streets. Bright was also an enthusiast for Pitman's shorthand!

**Brontë Street**
This is one of several streets with Brontë interest. The Reverend Patrick Brontë BA took up residence in Haworth Parsonage in February 1820, having moved his wife and six children, with seven cartloads of furniture (or two flatcarts, depending which version you prefer), to Haworth from Thornton, a small hillside village on the outskirts of Bradford.

Ghostly goings-on at an antique shop in Brontë Street were reported by the Keighley News in November 1976, including sightings of a uniformed soldier, noises on the stairs and flying saucers and clocks!

See Appendix for some other streets with Brontë interest.

**Brow Road/ Brow Top Road**
Haworth Brow was noted in the 1684 Parish Registers. The word comes from the Old English word for the brow of a hill, or a

*Bridgehouse Lane. Brow Road can be seen in the distance leading steeply up to Hebden Bridge Road.*

forehead or edge - in fact, Brow Road's precipitous gradient must make it one of the steepest in a region of steep streets. Haworth Brow side streets and houses were laid down from 1860 to 1880 onwards, in small lots, as housing was needed for mill workers with the expansion of the worsted industry. Brow Top was an area of common land, being recorded in the 1853 Tithe Awards, and Brow Top Farm dates from 1699. Houses, land and crofts around Haworth Brow were owned in 1838 by Joseph and John Wright Greenwood, and by Michael Pighills.

The quarries on Brow Moor provided stone for the workers' houses built at Brow. E.J. Emmott Esq. was granted permission for a new road at Brow, in 1904.

A section of the Blue Bell and Toller Lane turnpike, the road continues over the moor to Flappit and Cullingworth.

## Butt Lane

There are at least three possible meanings, each very different: the Old English word for a tree stump, Middle English for the strip of land adjoining a boundary in the common fields or from an Old French word for a mound, especially for archery practice! The original Butt Field was on the opposite side of Butt Lane to the park (Ref. 65, 1852 Tithe Award), and in 1838, along with Acre, was owned by Hiram Craven and tenanted by Hiram Hartley.

Haworth School Board was given planning permission for new streets in September 1895, and the New Central Schools (Butt Lane) one month later.

## Carlton Street

Parallel to Dean Street, Carlton Street also dates from the latter half of the nineteenth century. The Carlton club was a political (Conservative) club founded in the West End of London in 1831.

*Butt Lane.*

## Cecil Street

Lord Robert Cecil (Robert Arthur Talbot Gascoigne-Cecil, 3rd Marquis of Salisbury (1830 - 1903), was a Conservative politician who became Foreign Secretary and three times Prime Minister – the first time in 1885, after the murder of General Gordon at Khartoum contributed to the defeat of Gladstone. Salisbury supported Cecil Rhodes in Central Africa, and was devoted to foreign affairs, protecting and extending the colonies during his office. It was he who finally signed the peace treaty with the Boers in 1902. He has been described as the 'spirit' of the Victorian age.

In addition, the street may be named for Cecil John Rhodes (1853 - 1902), one of the great Victorian figures of empire. His driving force was for the extension of the British Empire as a great power throughout the world, and as a result to make wars impossible. Noting the proximity to Gordon Street, it is interesting that Cecil Rhodes met General Charles G. Gordon in Basutoland, and the latter tried to persuade Rhodes to leave South Africa and work with him. Cecil Rhodes became prime minister of the Cape in 1890. The former colonial territory of 'Rhodesia' now Zambia, was named after him.

*Junction of Changegate and West Lane – the Tourist Information Centre, formerly the Yorkshire Penny Bank*

See also other Lees streets on the theme of exploration and empire: Albion Street, Douglas Street, Gordon Street, Nares Street, Nile Street, Stanley Street.

## Changegate (Change Gate)

There may be a Saxon site on the corner of Change gate and North Street. Formerly known as Ginnel, Change Gate begins

31

at the building which is now the Tourist Information Centre, formerly the Yorkshire Penny Bank. It is thought that the name (first listed on the Census of 1881) refers to the exchange of money - particularly as the Yorkshire Penny Bank stood on the corner.

## Church Street

Emily Brontë's poem refers to, 'A little and a lone green lane, that opened on a common wide'.

A visitor to the Brontë Parsonage would be likely to walk up cobbled Church Street (previously Parsonage Lane) from the Tourist Information Centre, passing on the left the Church of St. Michael and All Angels and on the right the former National School (Sunday School) where Charlotte, Anne and Branwell Brontë taught. Passing the Parsonage and Museum on the left, the visitor finally steps out onto the path in a westerly direction across sloping fields towards Penistone Hill and the moors.

Parts of the Church tower are said to date from the fourteenth century, and the celebrated Reverend Grimshaw enlarged the Church in 1755. It is said that this evangelistic clergyman would begin a service with a particularly long hymn, and then leave the Church to drive out the drinkers in the local inns, to join the service. At his invitation, John Wesley preached at the Church in 1748, and his service began at 5 a.m., later preaching to a congregation of 4,000 in the graveyard. It is said that some

*The Parsonage is on the left.*

*Clarendon Street. House with inscription over the door.*

40,000 people lie buried in the graveyard, and the practice of burning coffins took place when the Churchyard became too full, filling the air with acrid fumes.

In the Reverend Brontë's time, the Church was very dilapidated, and most of it was later demolished and rebuilt (1879).

## Clarendon Street

George Villiers, 4th Earl of Clarendon, was Queen Victoria's Principal Secretary of State for Foreign Affairs. He was famous for sending the despatch from Paris announcing the peace treaty which ended the war in the Crimea.

## Cliff Street

The name is from the Old English for a steep bank or river bank. Cliff Street dates from the late 1870's. Robert Feather built 8 back to back houses in 1877-78. When William Gott applied for permission to build 41 houses on Cliff Street and Norman Street, he was refused because the building line had been altered from the estate plan and because he had not allowed sufficient width in the passages to allow for the drain being easily cleansed. Many of the Brow planning applications were refused because the speculators wanted to cram too many streets and houses in the space available - or because the terrain was too steep.

### Cold Street

The old field name Coldshaw means 'cold' and 'a small wood'. Cold Street leads out across Cold Shaw Fields to Old Oxenhope. This isolated path out of the village and across the fields was used by workers going to the mill. The story is that the mill workers carried jam jars, with a candle in to light their way.

Off Cold Street are rows of stone terraces, all built around the same time, with the unusual names of colours: Green Street, Pink Street, Rose Street, Violet Street.

Joseph Ogden of Coldshaw was given planning permission to build houses in Coldshaw, Pink and Rose Streets in 1889 and 1891 and Willie Howker for 3 houses in 1888. In 1899, William Brown of the Manor House applied for planning permission to build new streets at Coldshaw, but was refused because his streets were only 30ft wide. He was forced to amend the width to 36ft and permission was then given.

### Dean Street

Plunging recklessly down the Brow hillside, Dean Street is heading for its appropriate assumed meaning 'valley'.

Dean Street dates from the latter half of the nineteenth century. Permission was given in 1887 for Messrs D. Gott and Co. to build 12 dwelling houses on Dean, Duke and Lord Streets. In 1891, F. Dingby of Belle Isle was able to build a house and

*Dean Street.*

*Dimples Lane, looking toward the moors route over the Pennines.*

shop on Dean and Carlton Streets.

On a different theme, Ellen Dean is Mr. Lockwood's housekeeper in *Wuthering Heights*.

### Dimples Lane

The name 'dympel' means a deep hole or pit, or even a pool in a wood or dell. Stone quarrying was an essential industry in Haworth, and the lane served two quarries, Dimples and Penistone. There are two large fields named Dimples very close to Dimples End Quarry on the 1852 Tithe Award field map. The Emmott family (the late Richard) owned land and property in this area in 1838 - including Belle Isle and the Corn Mill. There were in the past as many as eight quarries working on the Haworth moors.

See Emmot Farm Fold for more details of the Emmotts.

### Douglas Street

David Douglas was a Scottish botanist (1798 - 1834) who explored California and the Fraser river region for the Royal Horticultural Society, bringing back from there and from British Columbia many new trees, shrubs and plants. He died far from home in the Sandwich Islands. Douglas Street may therefore have the right to be included in the group of Lees streets named after explorers.

A further choice is Sir James Douglas (1803 - 1877), Governor of Vancouver Island and British Columbia, who achieved distinction by maintaining British rule during the 1858 gold rush.

Also a Scottish noble family name, the two elements form the meaning 'black stream', from pre-English and British words.

See also other Lees streets on the themes of exploration and empire: Albion Street, Cecil Street, Gordon Street, Nares Street, Nile Street, Stanley Street.

## Dove Street

The name, apart from referring to the native bird, is a pre-English word which described streams and rivers, meaning 'black'. There are several other Haworth streets named after native birds.

See Appendix for some other names, e.g. Jay Street, Lawcliffe Crescent and Wren Street.

## Drill Street

Like Surgery Street, this is an example of a street named after a notable building along it. The Haworth army volunteers used a large drill shed from 1870 - later it was rebuilt as the Army Drill Hall, and was the base for a unit of the 6th Volunteer Battalion, the Duke of Wellington's West Riding Regiment.

## Duke Street

A number of Haworth streets are named after royalty. See Appendix for others.

## Eagle Street

Eagles may have once been present throughout England (except in the east), from the numbers of place names which incorporate the word.

See Appendix for some other Haworth streets named after birds.

## Earl Street

This was the name for an Anglo Saxon nobleman and also an Old English personal name. After the Norman conquest, 'Earl' came to be used as a title.

See Appendix for some other Haworth streets named after royalty.

## East Terrace

This Victorian row at Lees, leads out in an easterly direction, onto the moor.

*Junction of Earl Street and Ivy Bank Lane.*

### Ebor Lane
The word ebor is often found in this area, and means a wild boar. Wild boar would be common throughout the wooded parts of Britain before clearances and hunting gradually drove them out. The lane was a Private Occupation Road, owned by John Craven of Berridge House in Bingley in the nineteenth century. At the Mytholmes end there was a Toll Bar, and a Toll House which still exists, although no tolls have been levied since the 1930s.

### Emily Street
The back to back houses on Emily Street dated from 1880.

See Appendix, for Haworth streets relating to girls' names, and Brontë interest.

### Emmot Farm Fold
The British Kingdom of Elmet, which fell to Saxon invaders after 616 AD, is believed to have been the land between the rivers Aire and Wharfe, and this could have been the origin of the old established local family name of Emmot or Emmott. It actually means 'waters meet' in Old English.

The Old Hall is often referred to as Emmott Hall. The Emmotts were a landowning family whose residence was Emmott Hall at Laneshaw Bridge over the border in Lancashire. They owned the Old Hall and land in the Haworth area for a considerable time, up to the nineteenth century.

See also Old Hall Close, Hall Street.

### Fairfax Street

Sir Thomas Fairfax (1612-1671), celebrated in the pamphlet 'The Rider of the White Horse' was a Yorkshire Parliamentarian and hero of the Civil War. He led the Bradford resistance to the Earl of Newcastle's massive army, in December 1642, and was famous throughout the country.

Fairfax is also the middle name of Mr Edward Rochester in Charlotte Brontë's *Jane Eyre*.

### Fallwood Street

The name means 'a forest clearing', with reference to felling trees in a wood (Old English). Fall Wood was a field name at Haworth Brow. In 1838 it belonged to James Greenwood, the tenant being George Sunderland. Parker's Fallwood Brewery (Brow Road) also commemorates the name!

Fellwood Avenue and Close are not far away, off Vale Mill Lane, and mean the same.

### Fern Street

The old buildings on Fern Street date from the seventeenth and eighteenth centuries, and would overlook the Hall Green. The house at no. 8 Fern Street (10 Clarendon Street) is dated 1724.

See Appendix for some other Haworth streets named after plants.

*Fern Street.*

## Fife Street

Planning permission was given to Richard Sunderland for two blocks of back to back dwelling houses or 8 houses on Fife Street, in 1887.

## Fir Street

Built in the 1880's, Fir Street is one of a number of Haworth streets named after trees.

See Appendix for some others.

## Folly View Road

The road looks straight across the valley to Folly Field (Ref 387, 1852 Tithe Award). Folly Field House first appears on the 1871 Census, although a blacksmith's shop at Folly, owned by John Uttley, is listed in the 1838 Survey. This is quite appropriate as the word comes from Old Norse, meaning 'foal'. The folly was the local name for Ivy Bank Mills.

## Frith Street

Another reference to woodlands, this Old English word indicates an extensive region of woods.

However, turning to Victorian times, two famous Friths were the photographer Francis Frith, whose 'picture postcard' photographs of town and village scenes were sold widely, and William Powell Frith, the much admired panorama painter.

*The entrance to Gauger's Croft can still be seen leading off Main Street.*

## Gas Street

Not surprisingly, this tiny street pointed helpfully to the gas works (built in 1851), situated on the plot of land between Apsley Street and Prince Street.

## Gauger's Croft

The name possibly comes from the activity of excise men who would need to check wines and spirits stored in the Croft's buildings. 'Brandy Row' was a group of three rows of terraces on the edge of the Croft. Textile and other workers lived in filthy and overcrowded conditions in a warren of streets, yards and store buildings, condemned by the Babbage Report of 1850. Gauger's Croft no longer exists, but it is still possible to see the narrow entrance from Main Street.

Streets which have been demolished include Cork Street, Moon Street, Mount Street, Roper Street and Star Street.

### Gillstone Drive
The first part of the word is from an old Scandinavian word for 'ravine'.

### Gordon Street
General Charles George Gordon (1883 - 1885) was a spirited British military leader, and hero of the Victorian public. He led the defence of Khartoum for ten months, tragically in vain, as the relief forces arrived three days too late, with Gordon already dead.

Nicknamed 'Chinese Gordon' (due to a period in command of Chinese troops), he served in the Crimean War and was Governor of the Sudan, where he tried to suppress slave trading. He also led expeditions to explore and map the river Nile (between 1874 and 1877). He was a true visionary hero of his age.

See Appendix, for other Lees streets on the theme of exploration and empire, e.g. Albion Street, Cecil Street, Nares Street, Nile Street and Stanley Street.

### Green Street
An unusually named group of Haworth streets refer to colours: others are Pink Street, Rose Street and Violet Street.

### Greenfield Terrace
Greenfield Terrace, off Mytholmes Lane, is named after Greenfield House located nearby along a track. Greenfield appears on the 1851 census. James Bottomley was given planning permission in 1899 to build 17 houses forming numbers 8 - 40 Mytholmes Lane (Greenfield Terrace), and the following year, 8 houses. J.H. Pickles of Haworth then had a chance to slip in permission for 2 cottages at Greenfield in 1900.

## Hall Street

Hall Street is built on the site of Hall Green Fold - on an open green which lay below the Old Hall, and which was later built over with streets of houses for textile workers. Hall Green Baptist Chapel, in a prominent position across the road from the Old Hall, was built in 1825.

See also Old Hall Close.

## Heath-Cliff

Named for Heathcliff in Emily Brontë's *Wuthering Heights*, this modern housing development gained a civic award. It is also fitting that the heath plant (Erica tetralix) grows as a wild native flower on the moors and cliffs, in full bloom in August.

## Hebden (Bridge) Road, Hebden Bridge Trust

The Lees to Hebden Bridge turnpike road dates from 1814. The Hebden Bridge Trust crossed the Blue Bell Trust at Haworth Brow, where there was a tollbar and toll house. 'Hebden' comes from Old English and means 'hip valley'.

## Ivy Bank Lane

Hophni Bland, who was in charge of his father's Ivy Bank Mill, built in the late 1870s, was granted planning permission for a dwelling house, stables and coach house at Ivy Bank in 1887. Ivy Bank Villa which at that time occupied the site, was listed as an uninhabited building on the 1871 census.

## Jane Street

This is one of a number of streets relating to female Christian names, with possible Brontë connections to Jane Eyre.

See Appendix, for other street names on the same themes.

## Janet Street

This is also one of a number of streets relating to female Christian names.

See Appendix for others.

## Jay Street

A group of streets at Haworth Brow are named after native birds: others listed on the 1891 Census are Dove Street, Lark Street, Rook Street and Wren Street.

See Appendix for other streets named after birds.

### Joggers Lane

Joggers Lane leads into old quarry workings, now a car park. The name is likely to refer to the Jagger family who came to work Bankfield Quarry around 1928 and employed up to 100 men, supplying building stone for Halifax and other towns. (The name may come from 'jaeger' which is a Saxon word meaning 'pedlar'.)

### King Street

Several streets are named after royalty: this one does not refer to a particular king.

See Appendix, for other Haworth streets named after royalty.

### Laburnum Grove

A number of Haworth streets are named after trees and plants.

See Appendix for others.

### Lawcliffe Crescent

The land belonged to Law House but this romantic name (directly from Old English) conjures up an image of larks swooping around a steep slope, riding the air currents. The larks still sing on Haworth moors.

See Appendix, for some other Haworth streets named after native birds, for example Dove Street, Jay Street and Wren Street.

### Lees Lane and Lees Bank Avenue, Hill, Drive, Road

The original meaning, from Old English, is a glade or clearing in a wood, and later, a pasture or meadow. A further meaning is a stream or bog.

### Lime Street

Lime Street may take its name from Lime Field, which lies further along Stubbing Lane (ref 645 in the Tithe Awards 1852). Lime, Stone and Sand streets are in close proximity, these being the basic building materials found in the area, to supply the Victorian builders.

### Linden Street

Linden means 'lime tree valley'. The large leafed lime has been found growing wild in the West Riding of Yorkshire and Herefordshire. In the distant past, the tree was far more common and was used in making rope and war shields. The name appears spelled as 'Lindon' on some maps.

## Little Street

Little Field appears on the Tithe Award (1852), very close to Little Street's cottages which were built in the first half of the nineteenth century.

## Lodge Street

This street owes its name to the Three Graces Lodge of Freemasons, which rented a meeting place there between 1833 and 1907. The street was previously known as Newell (or Newall) Hill. Newell is a local family name. Mark Newel (tailor) of Haworth is recorded as having lent a pair of scissors to Timothy Pickles for the

*Lodge Street.*

purpose of coin clipping – (on this occasion the deed was carried out in a wood at Mill Hey). The illegal activity of 'coining' (i.e. clipping the edges off gold coins, melting them down and making counterfeits) was widespread around Halifax in the eighteenth century.

## Longlands Drive

Longlands, now a Youth Hostel, was built in 1884 for Edwin Robinson Merrall, worsted manufacturer. The house has changed hands many times, being at different times a hostel for immigrant mill girls and an old people's home. The 'lands' part of the name has an additional Old Norse meaning of a small wood or grove - (possibly also having pagan religious associations).

## Lord Lane

The manors of Haworth and Harden, and with them the title of 'Lord of the Manor of Haworth' were bought in 1671 by William Midgley, and his son Joseph, of Haworth, from Nicholas Bladen of the Inner Temple, London. Haworth Church used to have a 'Lord's Pew', at the foot of which the Midgley family were buried.

*Lord Lane.*

At the top of Lord Lane, where it turns into Changegate, is the Manor House, which was owned by the lords of the manor and built in the early eighteenth century.

### Lord Street
This is one of a number of Haworth streets named after royalty.

See Appendix for others.

### Lune Street
This river name means 'health giving water', from an Irish word, or 'full' in Welsh. It is curious that river names from before the Saxon conquest have often survived in use, unlike the place names, and it is often difficult to discover their original meaning.

See Appendix for other streets with a river theme.

### Main Street
The steep stone-setted Main Street, the main thoroughfare before the bypass was built, is lined with grey stone cottages,

44

many of which were once the homes of handloom weavers, hand woolcombers and spinners. The handloom was in the top storey, which had particularly large windows to admit the maximum amount of light. There were over 1000 looms in the village before the mills took over. The shops gradually grew in number as textile workers moved out.

The 6-inch stone setts (laid edgeways to prevent weathering), were supplied by the Jaggers' Quarry when the main street was

*Main Street.*

relaid in the 1930s. Ten ton loads of stone were seen being transported down the precipitous main street (which has a gradient of 1 in 6 in places) by waggons and horses at the turn of the century.

Main Street has also been known as the Village Street (1841 census), Brigg Lane (below the Fleece Inn), Low Street and Kirkgate (from above the Fleece Inn to the Church gates).

The turnpike road from Blue Bell, just outside Colne to Toller Lane, Bradford, continued down Main Street to the two Toll Bars at the junction of Sun Street and Bridgehouse Lane.

## May Street

This is one of a number of Haworth streets relating to female Christian names.

See Appendix for others.

## Mill Hey

Mill Hey was once called Milne Hey (1690), meaning mill enclosure or hedge. The mill in question refers to an ancient (possibly medieval) corn mill, which is said to have stood on what is now the station yard. Mill Hey used to be a part of Syke (or Sike) Lane, (which means a watercourse). The 1847 survey shows Mill Hill linking what is now Acre Lane with Sike Lane (now Belle Isle Road). Syke Field (Ref. 580, 1852 Tithe Award) lies just off Syke Lane.

Other fields with names linking to road names nearby were Milner Bank, Upper Hey Head, Lee Syke Field, Upper Hey and Lower Hey. Many people with the surname Hey are listed in the Tithe Award.

## Minnie Street

This is one of a number of Haworth streets relating to female Christian names. The Royal Woodlands Lodge obtained permission to build 5 houses on Minnie Street in 1887, and Miss Gregson to build semi-detached houses in 1889.

See Appendix, for other streets on the same theme.

## Mytholmes Lane

Previously Mytholme Lane, the name Mythomes is recorded in 1639 (Court Rolls of Haworth), and has the meaning 'where streams join'. Other spellings are Mythams (1546), Michams and Mithams. This is very appropriate as the River Worth and the Bridgehouse Beck join close by. Another interpretation is that the word comes from Norse, meaning 'middle fenny ground' - and could therefore indicate Norse settlement in the area. Tolls were collected at the Toll Bar House on Mytholmes Lane (which is listed in the 1845 Township Rate Book) until 1935.

Planning permission was given to G. Hattersley and Son to build new streets and a further 13 houses at Mytholmes in 1889 (previous permission was in 1878 for 12 houses). In 1898, Messrs Hattersley were able to build a further 16 houses, James Bottomley of Prince Street was granted permission for new streets and A. Simpson of Bradford for two houses.

Plans for Haworth UDC, for 20 houses for a housing scheme at Mytholmes, were passed in March 1927.

*Mytholmes Lane – Toll House. The stone plaque refers to a Private Occupation Road between Oakworth Hall and Ebor Lane Top.*

## Nares Street

Nares Street is one of a group of streets at Lees interestingly named after Victorian explorers. Sir George Strong Nares (1831 - 1915) was a Scottish sea captain who commanded HMS Challenger on exploratory voyages to the Arctic, Antarctic, Australia and South America.

See also other Lees streets on the theme of exploration and empire: Albion Street, Arctic Street, Cecil Street, Douglas Street, Gordon Street, Stanley Street, Nile Street (also listed in Appendix)

## Nelson Street

The British Admiral, Horatio Viscount Nelson (1758 - 1805), created Duke of Brontë (by the king of Naples) in 1799, was a hero said to be much admired by the Reverend Patrick Brontë, (who was pleased to change his own name from Brunty). Lord Nelson was fatally wounded and died in the victory of Trafalgar, after a glittering naval career.

The proximity of Arctic Street recalls Nelson's early service at the age of fifteen, on an expedition to the arctic region in the 'Carcass', under the command of Captain Phipps. His next expedition was to the East Indies (which coincides with East Terrace - the third street in this small Lees group!). There may also be a link in the mind of the street-namer with Nile Street, recalling Nelson's famous victory on the Nile in 1798.

See also: Arctic Street, Nares Street.

## New Holme Road

The word 'holme' comes from an Old Scandinavian word for 'a piece of dry ground in a marsh' or 'a water meadow'. Nearby, along Bridgehouse Beck, lie fields named Holme, Round Holme, Rushy Holme, Bracken Holme and Great Holme (Tithe Award 1852).

## New Street

This street is probably named after the New Inn, (also known as the 'Stubbin Pub') which was a little further along Sun Street, towards Oxenhope, and closed in the 1930's. There is an old, unpalatable story about the landlord of the New Inn who once served up rat pie as a free hot supper. This happened after the rat catcher had been and did not know what to do with his catch. It was not a popular dish.

*Nile Street.*

## Nile Street

The source of the river Nile was discovered in 1862 by J.H. Speke. Other famous explorers who continued to explore and map the river over the next twenty years were General C.G. Gordon (of Khartoum) and H.M. Stanley. Lake Victoria was discovered and named in honour of the Queen by J.H. Speke (in 1858) and Lake Albert was honourably named soon after by Sir Samuel Baker.

See also other Lees streets on the theme of exploration and empire: Albion Street, Cecil Street, Douglas Street, Gordon Street, Nares Street, Stanley Street (also listed in Appendix).

## Norbreck Drive

The two elements of the name are from the Old English meaning 'north' and 'new land taken into cultivation'.

## Norman Street

George Warde Norman was a financier whose views were instrumental in the formation of the Bank Charter Act of 1844. The first provincial joint-stock banks had been formed at Huddersfield and Bradford in 1827.

## North Street

Formerly Back Lane (a common name given to a street which ran at the back of houses), North Street forms the northern boundary of the main group of streets and houses at the top of the town. In 1895 Messrs Merralls of Haworth were granted permission for a new street or continuation of North Street. There was a flurry of planning permissions in 1896-97, with building applications approved to Messrs Sutcliffe and Kendal of West Lane, Mrs Shackleton of West Lane, James Pedley of West Lane and Merrall and Son of Haworth.

## Oak Street

A number of streets are named after trees and shrubs. Oak Street was the home of Ogden's Brewery, and also serves as a reminder of the oak casks used for storing ale. It dates from 1890.

See Appendix, for other Haworth streets named after trees.

## Old Hall Close

The Old Hall dates from at least Elizabethan times, and is believed to be the site of an even older hall and church, dating back to the Normans, and the traditional seat of the Squires of Haworth. It is said that there are two underground escape passages - one leading to the Church (or the wine cellar of the Black Bull) and one leading to Bridge House, but this has never been verified. Also known as Emmott Hall, the Old Hall is said to be haunted and that the cellars once served as a burial ground when the buildings belonged to a religious house around the fifteenth century. Ghost legends include sightings of a monk in a blue haze seen walking through the kitchen wall and a little girl in a crinoline dress. The Old Hall was also known as Sagar Fold in the nineteenth century, this being the name of the tenant farmers.

Hall Field was the adjacent land belonging to the Old Hall, lying between there and Balcony House (Ref. 309, 1852 Tithe Award).

See also Emmot Farm Fold, Hall Street.

## Oldfield Lane

The name 'Oldfield' appears in 1650 (Parish Registers of Haworth), with later references to Oldfield Gate. The word means 'open country', and this usually means heathland, which has been forested, but is now cleared.

## Ouse Street
The river Ouse flows into the Humber. There are several possible meanings, the options being water (Celtic), mud, wet or winding (Old English).

See Appendix, for other Haworth streets with a river theme.

## Park Street
Shown as leading to a small wooded area on the 1892 map, planning permission for 5 houses was given to Booth and Holmes in 1890, and Messrs J. and J. Moore of Main Street were allowed to build 16 houses on Park and Gladstone Streets between 1893 and 1895.

## Pink Street
A small group of streets off Cold Street is unusually named after colours. Others are Rose Street and Violet Street. Perhaps one could imagine fancifully that these are sunset hues, as the streets point generally west towards the sunset!

## Portland Street
The name comes from the Latin for a harbour or gateway. A massive naval defence task in Dorset in the mid nineteenth century, was the construction of Portland's breakwaters, enclosing the great roadstead of Portland harbour. The breakwaters were built by convicts from 1847-62.

Portland stone was a limestone quarried at Portland, and used in the construction of many fine buildings. A process for making 'Portland cement' (so called because it was thought to resemble the famous stone) was patented by Joseph Aspdin in 1824. A famous 'Portland' was Henry Cavendish Bentinck, 3rd Duke of Portland, who was Prime Minister in 1783 and 1807-09. Duke Street is also close by.

## Prince Street
The name may refer to Prince Albert, but many Victorian streets were named after 'royalty' without meaning a particular individual (see also Duke Street, Lord Street). It is interesting to chart the development of the street through the different speculators and builders who were granted planning permission for houses.

51

Five cottages were built on Prince and Aire Streets by J.W. and R. Sunderland in 1884, and William Brown submitted his amended plan and section of the street in 1886. William Sunderland had plans passed for five dwelling houses and a shop in 1887, with two houses and a shop in 1888. However, later that year Richard Sunderland was refused permission to build a block of four houses, 'because the width of the back street is not in accordance with Section 8 of the Haworth Local Byelaws.'

In 1890, plans were passed for eight back to back houses for J. Smith, and one house for William Brown.

1891 saw a successful submission for 8 houses from Edmund Brown. However, also in 1891, a plan was put forward by John Rhodes and Sons, Mill Hey, for 15 houses on Ouse and Prince Streets. This was refused because '...the block plan is not in accordance with the estate plan and the buildings are not set back to the building line prescribed by the Board...the air space is not exclusive by belonging to each house in accordance with Section 22 of the Act.'

In 1892 plans for further houses were passed for Messrs G. Taylor and H. Stanley, Richard Sunderland of Oxenhope, Thomas Bottomley of Haworth and William Brown.

Sam Ogden of Oak Street received approval for six houses and a shop on Prince and Apsley Streets in 1897.

In 1898, James Bottomley of Prince Street had plans passed for fourteen cottages on Norman and Prince Streets and Messrs Lister, Moore and Denby for six houses. Finally, plans by Samuel Ogden, Fallwood Street, for eleven houses were accepted in 1903.

**Prospect Street**
There are 'Prospect Streets' in many nineteenth century groups of streets in towns and cities. Usually (as in Haworth) there is a park or other pleasant view in the vicinity. It is also an example of a name celebrating Victorian civic pride and hope for the future. Prospect Street was laid down in the early nineteenth century John Hartley obtained permission to build five more dwelling houses in 1887.

**Rawdon Road**
Rawdon Road forms a byepass so that the historic Main Street can have restricted access. When excavations were carried out in

the new car park, a seventeenth century stone lined well was found, fed by a spring. This was near Well Street, a demolished street in Gauger's Croft. Also found was an underground river, and a road with small setts, which was thought to be an extension of a setted road uncovered near the railway footbridge. Rawdon is from Old Norse words for 'red hill'. Captain Rawdon lived in the Old Hall on Sun Street. In 1893 he was successful in obtaining planning permission to build three privies at the Hall!

### Regent Street

Many Haworth streets are named after royalty. James Bottomley of Greenfield (previously of Prince Street), obtained permission to build twenty three houses on Regent Street in 1904.

See Appendix, for other streets with the same theme.

### River Street

Little River Street, laid down in the latter half of the nineteenth century, leads down to Bridgehouse Beck. Close by there are two river named streets, Aire Street and Ouse Street.

See Appendix for other streets with the same theme.

### Roper Street

Roper was an established family name in the area. A worsted manufacturing family of this name built Damems Mill, further down the valley. This street was demolished with Gauger's Croft.

### Rose Street

A small group of streets off Cold Street is unusually named after colours. Others are Pink Street and Violet Street.

### Rosslyn Grove

Planning permission was given for fourteen houses on Rosslyn Grove in March 1938.

### Ruth Street

This is one of a number of streets relating to female Christian names. This may be a Biblical reference to the Book of Ruth in the Old Testament, taking into account the proximity of Lees Church, Chapel and Sunday School.

See Appendix, for other street names on this theme.

**Sand Street**
See Lime Street

**Sedge Grove**
A number of streets bear the names of native trees and plants. This is an apt name as sedge likes to grow in damp places and the River Worth and Bridgehouse Beck flow nearby.

**Shirley Street**
Charlotte Brontë's novel *Shirley* was completed in 1849, a few months after Anne Brontë died in Scarborough, and it is said that Charlotte based the character Shirley on her sister Anne.

See Appendix, for other streets on themes of female Christian names and Brontë interest.

**South View**
South View takes its name from the house Southlands, which was used as the minister's house by the Wesleyan church in West Lane.

**Stanley Street**
Sir Henry Morton Stanley (1841 - 1904) was famous for his African exploration, and for finding the lost explorer David Livingstone at Lake Tanganyika in 1871. He is then reputed to have delivered the memorable words 'Dr Livingstone, I presume?'. He led expeditions which confirmed the source of the river Nile (between 1874 and 1877), explored the river Congo and found the Mountains of the Moon.

See Appendix, and other Lees streets on the theme of exploration and empire, for example Albion Street, Cecil Street, Gordon Street, Nares Street and Nile Street

**Station Road**
This road, taking in the station forecourt, connected Mill Hey to Bridgehouse Lane. It was built when the railway's arrival cut off access to Belle Isle Road. The Worth Valley Railway, which is a single track running the five miles between Oxenhope and Keighley, was commenced in 1864 and opened on the 13th April, 1867.

**Stone Street**
See Lime Street

## Stubbing Lane (Sun Lane)

The former name for Sun Lane, Stubbing Lane is one of the few named on the 1852 map. The name comes from the Old English word for tree stump, and implies that the area was cleared of trees, perhaps leaving stumps visible. 'Woodlands', the mill owner's house built at the beginning of the nineteenth century, adds to the tree references in this area.

## Sun Street

*Sun Street was previously Stubbing Lane, to Stubbing Gate.*

At the junction of Sun Street and Cold Street, was the ducking pond where the Scold's Stool or 'Scalping Stool' was situated. Those to be strapped into the ducking chair and dipped included men and women scolds, brawling women, dishonest bakers and disturbers of the peace! The pond, later built as a well, was first located in the centre of the three roads, and then by the side of Sun Street (but did not have water in it from about 1910).

Many of the cottages on Sun Street date from the early nineteenth century. William Brown of the Manor House successfully applied for planning permission for new streets, off Sun Street, in 1898.

Sun Croft, however, is a strip of field behind the Sun Inn, on West Lane (Ref. 320, 1852 Tithe Award).

## Surgery Street

When a visit to the doctor was needed in the late nineteenth century, his surgery was located along Surgery Street, at the side of Bridge House.

*Sun Street. Site of the Ducking Stool.*

### Thomas Street

As well as a Christian name, Thomas was a local surname. Enoch Thomas was innkeeper of the King's Arms on Church Street (Parsonage Lane) in 1841, and in the 1838 Survey and Valuation a William Thomas owned Chapel Field (next to Parson's Croft and Parson Field).

### Tim Lane

The 1741 Parish Register relates how 'one of the duties of the Clerk is to ring the great bell at 8 a.m. every Sunday, announcing thereby the day of the month, by causing the bell to strike as many times as days'. There were formerly three bells in Haworth steeple, the third being purchased in 1741 and named 'Great Tim'.

### Tulip Street

Tulip seeds were first exported to Austria from Turkey in the mid sixteenth century. The first cargos of bulbs were transported from Istanbul to Antwerp in 1562.

### Victoria Road (Haworth Brow), Victoria Avenue (Mytholmes)

Born on May 24, 1819, Victoria was Queen of the United Kingdom of Great Britain and Ireland from 1837, and also Empress of India from 1876. Her reign was the longest in English history, encompassing tremendous changes and advances in science, technology, exploration and the arts. She restored popularity to the crown and died at Osborne in the Isle of Wight on January 22 1901, being buried beside her beloved Prince Albert at Frogmore near Windsor.

### Violet Street

A small group of streets off Cold Street is unusually named after colours. Others are Pink Street and Rose Street.

### Weavers Hill

It is estimated that in 1838 there were 1,200 hand looms in Haworth engaged in worsted weaving.

### West Lane

The lane leading west out of Haworth towards the moors and Colne is the old Haworth and Blue Bell Trust (or Toller Lane, which reached Bradford in the other direction). Stage coaches followed this wild road to climb across the Pennines, through Stanbury and Scartop, up past the Herders Inn and down to Laneshaw Bridge in Lancashire. The Toll Bar on the approach to Haworth was placed across the road at the Sun Inn. This turnpike road crossed the Lees to Hebden Bridge Trust at Haworth Brow.

West Lane cottages numbered from 19 to 33, date from the early nineteenth century. An amended building line and plan of 15 houses and new streets, for Messrs Wood and Thornton, West Lane, was passed in 1903.

## Woodlands Rise

The name celebrates Woodlands, the large mill owner's house which dates from the first part of the nineteenth century, being listed in the Rate Book for 1833. In the 1836 Survey and Valuation of the Township of Haworth, the Greenwood family were owner occupiers and tenants of Woodlands. James Greenwood was a worsted manufacturer and landowner, who was made bankrupt in 1848. In the 1891 Census, Woodlands was the home of John Ramsden Redman, worsted spinner and manufacturer.

The name of Woodlands also descibes the locality where woods were cleared away to provide fields.
See also Stubbing Lane.

## Wren Street

This is one of several streets named after birds which may be found in this area.

Richard Sunderland was granted permission to build 4 houses on Wren Street in 1889. See Appendix, for other streets named after birds, for example Dove Street and Jay Street.

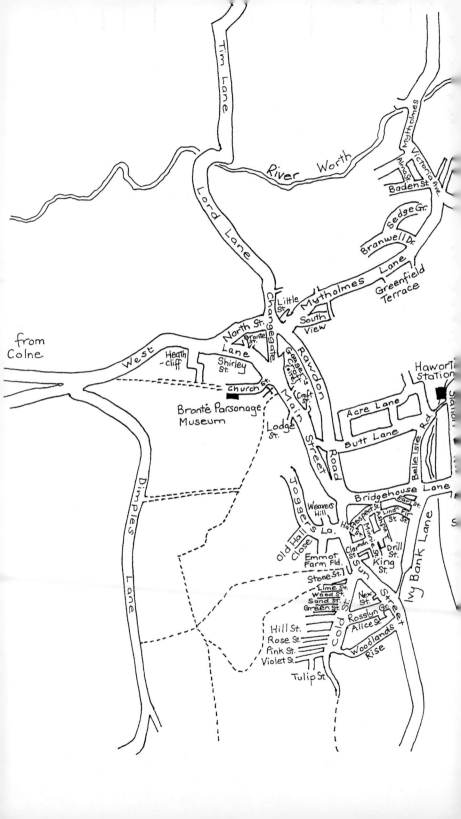

# *Appendix*

## Examples of themed street names.

Note that some of these Haworth streets no longer exist.

*Names relating to trees*
Ash Street
Ashfield Terrace
Fir Street
Lime Street
Linden Street
Oak Street
Pine Street

*Names relating to colours*
Green Street
Pink Street
Rose Street
Violet Street

*Names relating to rivers*
Aire Street
Lune Street
Ouse Street
River Street
Tyne Street

*Names relating to birds*
Dove Street
Eagle Street
Jay Street
Lark Street
Lawcliffe Crescent
Rook Street
Wren Street

*Names relating to girls' Christian names*
Ann Street
Janet Street
May Street
Minnie Street
Ruth Street
Shirley Street

*Names relating to plants*
Fern Street
Ivy Bank Lane
Laburnum Grove
Sedge Grove
Tulip Street

*Names relating to Queen Victoria and Royalty*
Alice Street
Duke Street
Lord Street
Prince Street
Queen Street
Victoria Avenue, Road

*Names relating to historical events and famous people*
Albion Street
Alma Street
Baden Street
Bright Street
Clarendon Street
Fairfax Street
Frith Street
Gordon Street
Nares Street
Nile Street
Stanley Street

*Some possible Brontë references*
Acton Street (now demolished)
Ann Street
Branwell Drive
Bronte Street
Emily Street
Heath-Cliff
Jane Street
Shirley Street

# Bibliography

Babbage, Benjamin Herschel. *Report to the General Board of Health on a Preliminary Inquiry into the Sewerage, Drainage and Supply of Water, and the Sanitary Condition of the Inhabitants of the Hamlet of Haworth, in the West Riding of the County of York.* 1850.

Baumber, M.L. *From Revival to Regency: a History of Keighley and Haworth 1740 - 1820.* Vol. 1. M.L. Baumber, 1983.

General Register Office Census 1841, 1851, 1861, 1871, 1881, 1891.

Davids, Shirley. *Haworth: Pictures from the Past.* 'Manorlands' and Shirley Davids, 1994.

Emsley, Kenneth. *Historic Haworth Today: an Illustrated Guide to the Historic Buildings and Families of Haworth, Stanbury, Oxenhope and the Worth Valley Railway.* Bradford Libraries, 1995.

Hartley, Marie and Ingilby, Joan. *Life and Tradition in West Yorkshire.* Smith Settle, 1990.

Haworth UDC. *Register of Building Plans, 1876 - 1938.*

Haworth Tithe Award, 1852 (with maps of village and fields, an abstract of the 1851 Census and field name and repopulation maps and index to tithe award. Transcribed from the map and award in the Sheepscar Record Office by L. and S. Wood).

Haworth Local Board of Health. *Haworth: Detail Plan. 1853.*

Haworth Society. *The Haworth Scene: Aspects of the Rural Community.*

Haworth Township Rate Books: 1833, 1834, 1836, 1842, 1843, 1845, 1848.

*Offices of the Haworth Local Board of Health. Minutes, 1871 - 1872.*

Ranger, William. 'Report to the General Board of Health on a further inquiry as to the boundaries which may be most advantageously adopted for the purposes of the Public Health Act, 1848, in the Parish of Haworth...' 1853.

Shepherd, Val. *Historic Wells In and Around Bradford.* Heart of Albion Press, 1994.

Smith, A.E. *Place Names of the West Riding.* English Place-Name Society, 1961.

Southwart, Elizabeth. *Brontë Moors and Villages from Thornton to Haworth,* 1923.

*Survey and Valuation of the Township of Haworth, 1838.*

T. Jefferys: *Maps of Yorkshire. 1771.*

Turner, J. Horsfall. *Haworth - Past and Present: a History of Haworth, Stanbury and Oxenhope.* J.S. Jowett, 1879.

Whynne-Hammond, Charles. *Tracing the History of Place Names.* Countryside Books, 1992.

# *A*cknowledgements

I would like to thank the following people for their help and encouragement in the street names project: Ian Dewhirst for his generous research advice, Bob Duckett of Bradford Libraries and the staff of Keighley Reference Library, for their professional interest and assistance, Chris Graham for his perceptive reading of the manuscript, Helen Broadhead of the Haworth History Society for her enthusiasm and support for the project. Mike Parsons of Wharncliffe Books, without whom this book would not have been written. My dear husband Roger for his patience and encouragement, Marjorie, for sending me to Arctic Street in a snowstorm. For being there – Pete, Mike, Kerri and Daniel.

Photographs on pages 5, 9, 24, 44, 45 and the illustration on page 19 are reproduced by kind permission of Bradford Libraries. All other photographs and illustrations were provided by the author.

# INDEX

63